Monographic Journals of the Near East Afroasiatic Linguistics 1/7 (March 1975)

This paper is part of the
Proceedings
of the
First North-American Conference on Semitic Linguistics
Santa Barbara, California
March 24-25, 1973

GRAPHEMICS AND DIACHRONY: SOME EVIDENCE FROM HEBREW CURSIVE

Harvey Minkoff
Hunter College of CUNY

The analysis of writing is shown to parallel that of speech. Graphemes--that is, letter shapes--are analyzed in terms of the physical distinctive features of strokes, minimal pairs, and etic and emic components. Hence, GRAPHEMICS.

In the development of Hebrew/Yiddish cursive from the medieval square forms, there is a clear tendency toward maximization of contrasts, elimination of redundancy, and evolution by means of drag chains and push chains; there is also some evidence of gradualness, and documentation of sub-emic change.

TABLE OF CONTENTS

0. INTRODUCTION

Writing systems as such are virtually ignored by modern American linguistics.[1] Likewise, most studies of writing ignore linguistic theory and methodology. Thus, while American linguists give considerable attention to possible evidence for phonology contained in written documents, they give little attention to writing as a proper linguistic system; and the otherwise fine descriptive and philological studies of writing generally overlook evidence significant to linguistic theory.[2] This is unfortunate, because a rigorous linguistic investigation of writing and written shapes can be productive of insights into both writing and linguistic theory.

For example, the study of the development of the various Hebrew writing systems has been marked by a great deal of very good descriptive work; but little has been attempted by way of discovering underlying linguistic principles motivating this development. For this reason, the evolution of non-scribal handwriting--generally called CURSIVE--is usually explained simply as the result of speed and carelessness. Yet, while this is certainly one part of the motivation, it does not in any way explain why the changes took the form that they did. The first part of this paper, therefore, is intended as a brief suggestion of how current linguistic methodology may illuminate aspects of the history of writing systems, in particular the evolution of the shapes of modern Hebrew/Yiddish cursive letters from the medieval square forms. The second part will discuss how these changes might be relevant to the larger concerns of diachrony in general.

1. EVOLUTION OF HEBREW/YIDDISH CURSIVE

1.1. Previous Interest in Graphemics

Weir (1967:170) notes that "it is not surprising that linguists have not paid too much attention to writing for some time. It was a difficult enough task to free ourselves from looking at language only through its written representation. . . . The victory of accepting the primacy of spoken language has in fact been won so hard that any concession to writing savored of retreat." Nonetheless, some linguists--most notably the functionalists--entertained high hopes during the 40's and 50's of finding parallels between phonemes and graphemes. Thus, Uldall (1944; 1966:147-148), citing Saussure's dictum that "language is form, not substance," argued that neither speech nor writing is primary since both are merely different substances of the language form, and even though the substance *ink* has not received as much attention as the substance *air*, "we can see at a glance, however, that it behaves in much the same way. . . . the shape of a letter varies according to the shape of neighboring letters, according to position in a group. . . , according to individual taste. . . ." Following Uldall, though noting that he "does not seem to have stressed sufficiently the autonomous character of written language," Vachek (1945-49:86-88) maintained that writing, like speech, is a system of signs of the first order, unlike phonetic transcription, which is a sign of the second

---

[1]As this paper develops ideas originally outlined in somewhat different form in Minkoff 1973a and 1973b, I wish to thank all those who commented on the earlier papers, especially Giorgio Buccellati, A.D. Corré, Talmy Givón, Robert Hetzron, Carlton Hodge, Samuel Levin, and Evelyn Melamed.

[2]Thus Kyes (1970:193) "...writing systems...were regarded as a means of recording phonological systems, and were of interest to the linguist only to the extent that they revealed, or were thought to reveal, an underlying phonological system." And Walsh (1964:519): "...the linguistic factors in alphabetic discussions have frequently been obscured and subordinated by historians of philological rather than linguistic bent."

order, and pointed out that "written language must be based on a system of graphic oppositions capable of differentiating meanings in the given community. And it is this system. . . which we call writing. The units of this system may be called graphemes. . . . Exactly as the phonemes of a given language are realized in concrete sounds and sound-attributes, so the graphemes become manifested in concrete letters and letter-attributes. . . ." And in this same vein, Pulgram (1951:15-16) outlined nine parallels between phonemes and graphemes, the most significant for this study being that by definition all phones/graphs identifiable as members of one phoneme/grapheme are its allophones/allographs; the phonetic/graphic shape of an allo is dependent on its producer and on its phonetic/graphic surroundings; dialects/alphabets are subject to phonemic/graphemic change and substitution.

But Bazell (1956; 1966:359), on the other hand, raised three objections to parallel analyses of writing and speech: one, that graphics is partially dependent on phonemics; two, that graphic systems vary, but phonemic ones are essentially similar; three, that graphics are relatively "artificial." And despite Vachek's belief (1945-49:93) that "the study of concrete writings and concrete written languages, as well as research in the theory of writing and of written language, is still in its infancy," the field's maturation was arrested, and the linguistic mainstream has since given little thought to most aspects of writing--the majority of the little that has been done being concerned with spelling, somewhat less with structure, and almost nothing with shape. Thus, Hockett (1958:539), for example, states that "though writing is not the linguist's primary concern, he is interested in it. . . [because] our records of the past. . . take the form exclusively of documents and inscriptions. . . ."[3] And Gleason (1961:409) merely summarizes the conclusions of the functionalists before devoting the rest of his chapter on writing to grapheme/phoneme "fit"--that is, whether the graphemes represent sound, syllables, or morphemes. Similarly, current interest centers almost exclusively on orthography (e.g., Weir 1967, Haas 1969, 1970, Venezky 1970), fit (e.g., Hill 1967), and structure (e.g., Vachek 1972). In fact, the one notable exception to this indifference to the behavior of the substance ink seems to be Eden 1961, which, however, is motivated not by linguistic concern per se but by the engineering problem of programming mechanical scanners. Yet Eden's exposition of the possibility of seeing individual handwritings in terms of objective distinctive features clearly has implications for linguistic research.[4]

1.2. Terminology

Since even in the few works cited there is a confusing difference in terminology, the terms used in the following discussion must be defined. Broadly speaking, CURSIVE is the non-professional form of Hebrew writing that developed from the artistic square-shaped letters of the professional scribes and illuminators. Though cursive occasionally appears in illuminated manuscripts--especially in marginal notes around a square-lettered text--it was more commonly used by scholars, merchants, and ordinary people for personal correspondence, contracts, and the like, since literacy was widespread among medieval Jews in Europe and North Africa. Cursive, therefore, is the type of lettering usually associated with "handwriting." GRAPHEMICS is the study of written shapes, with an eye to isolating the significant units, the GRAPHEMES.[5]

---

[3] Indeed, Kyes (199) remarks that "Hockett 1958 regarded writing as something that should be studied independently of linguistics."

[4] Apparently (and understandably) unaware of Eden's work, Hammarström (1964:333-4) says that a handwritten text cannot be segmented into letters by using minimal pairs or any other technique; his analyses are therefore based on the corresponding printed texts.

Also worth mentioning in passing is the irony that, as noted by Jakobson (1961a:245), the application of matematical communication theory to written language was one of the stimuli for the research that ultimately produced the concept of distinctive features in phonology.

[5] The term GRAPHEMICS is proposed here to emphasize that the parallel seems to be between graphemes and autonomous phonemes; GRAPHOLOGY, as used, for example, in Diringer 1962, is

Graphemes--often called letters--may be described in terms of their component STROKES, which are thus visual analogues to the distinctive features of phonology, and strokes are described in terms of length, shape, and location.[6] For example, English capital <H> is a grapheme composed of a regular straight left vertical, a regular straight right vertical, and a short straight mid horizontal. Capital <N> contrasts with <H> in one stroke, the diagonal, and the two are therefore in minimal contrast, or form a MINIMAL PAIR. The feature providing the minimal contrast for a set of graphemes is EMIC; all else is ETIC, or redundant. Analyzing the Hebrew square graphemes (fig.1) in this way shows that, in addition to number and location of strokes, graphemes minimally contrast on the basis of stroke length (fig. 2) and whether a corner is flush or overlapping (fig. 3). On the other hand, no minimal contrasts are based on curves--as in the English minimal pairs <O : D> and <U : V>--or solely on diagonals--as in <H : N>. In other words, stroke SHAPE IS ETIC and LENGTH AND TYPE OF CORNER ARE EMIC.

1.3. Analysis of Hebrew/Yiddish Cursive

This is significant when attempting to explain the particular changes that occurred in Hebrew/Yiddish cursive. For, though in many other areas cursive is little more than square graphemes with the corners rounded, in the Jewish communities of France and Germany and their daughter communities throughout Eastern Europe about half of the Hebrew cursive graphemes developed shapes that have little obvious resemblance to their square parents (fig. 4). Yet, if the squares are analyzed in terms of the emic and etic features just mentioned, the changes are seen to be extremely systematic. Moreover, comparison of the square and cursive graphemes shows that for any given grapheme two or more strokes not participating in emic contrasts are often reduced to etic curves or diagonals--or simply lost--while features in emic contrasts are never lost and are often exaggerated.

1.3.1. LOSS OF ETIC FEATURES

Consider, for example, the graphemes *koph*, *he*, *ḥeth*, and *tav* (fig. 5). All these graphemes share the features regular (straight) right vertical and regular (straight) high horizontal, but differ in their left component. Now, since--as we all know from personal experience--a major desire when writing is to finish as quickly as possible but still be able to read what is written;[7] and since in Hebrew, written from right to left, this means rushing to the left, it is clear that all four graphemes underwent the same change: reduction of etic components--which in these cases happen to be on the right--to curves or diagonals, and exaggeration of emic components--which happen to be on the left.

---

avoided since it suggests a parallel to modern phonology but the distinction between underlying representation and surface manifestation does not appear productive in graphemic analysis.

As used in Hammarström 1972 et al., graphemics is defined as spelling rules--"that part of linguistics...where units of the written language are described on the basis of their relation to units of the spoken language" (24). In Vachek 1945-49 and Pulgram 1951 it seems to include both letter shape and spelling; in Hockett 1958 this is called GRAPHONOMY.

Within the terminological frame proposed here, GRAPHEMES are the classes of significant shapes, as in Allén 1965, corresponding to Hammarström's TYPEMES. Consistent with their previous usage, Vachek and Pulgram use GRAPHEME for units of shape and spelling, as does Bazell 1956, while Hammarström uses it for units of spelling, analogous to Allén's PHONOGRAPHEME.

[6]Unlike both Bazel 1956 where each feature of a letter is considered equivalent to a phoneme, each letter to a morpheme, and each word to a sentence, and Eden 1961 where "the strokes are analogous to phonemes, the letters to morphemes and the words to words" (84).

[7]In this respect it is interesting to note that illegibility is much more common in the stylized cursive book-hands, sometimes called *mashait*, where speed and carelessness cannot be presumed. See below, the discussion of *'aleph*.

1.3.2. EXAGGERATION OF EMIC FEATURES

An interesting situation arises when an emic feature occurs on the *right* side of a grapheme, thus conflicting with the desired rapid movement leftward. As a matter of fact, the square alphabet has three pairs of graphemes in which a right corner is emic--flush *nun*, *kaph*, and *resh* contrasting with overlapping *gimmel*, *beth*, and *daleth* respectively--and in every case the same change evolved: the letter with the flush corner has simply rounded it, but the one with the overlapping corner has become completely distorted in the effort to quickly produce the emic feature (fig. 6). In addition, in every case the attempt to quickly produce an overlapping corner without lifting the pen resulted in the introduction of a short diagonal in stage 2 and a curve in stage 3--both etic features in Hebrew squares and thus easily added.

1.3.3. SYSTEMIC LOSS OF A FEATURE

Moreover, the additional loss of the short high horizontal stroke in both *nun* and *gimmel* seems to have been part of a systemic loss of that feature. As already noted (fig. 2), one series in the square alphabet contrasts REGULAR high horizontals with SHORT high horizontals: but no contrasting grapheme with NO high horizontal exists in this series. Since, of course, a distinction between NO stroke and ANY stroke is simpler, and therefore more efficient, than one between strokes of different lengths, the contrast was reinterpreted in the cursive script (fig. 7). And then, as can be seen, something like a drag chain developed--as short high strokes disappeared and regular ones became short allographically.

1.3.4. INTRODUCTION OF CURVES

An additional simple tendency that caused radical changes in the shapes of graphemes is the one that turned straight lines into loops because the writer failed to lift the pen while retracing a stroke. Since, as mentioned previously, there are no minimal pairs in the square alphabet based on curves, there was no danger of confusion if extra loops appeared, so long as the basic emic features were visible. This process has already been alluded to in the cases of *gimmel*, *beth*, and *daleth* (fig. 6); it also accounts for the changes in *shin* and *ᶜayin* (fig. 8). Because of the nature of the system, *shin* and *ᶜayin* were in minimal contrast in their square forms--two verticals being contrasted with three; the diagonal of the *ᶜayin* was purely etic, and, in fact, often appeared as a low horizontal or was virtually omitted, as in stage 2. This being so, it was easy enough to make the center vertical of *shin* as a continuation of the left-most vertical (stage 2), thereby producing the entire grapheme in one continuous stroke, and to make the second vertical of *ᶜayin* from the bottom of the first, later adding the loop of modern Hebrew/Yiddish cursive. A similar process seems to be behind the changes in both forms of cursive *ṣadhe* (fig. 9), which are really nothing more than trying to write the square forms with one stroke.

1.3.5. DEVELOPMENTS IN NONCONTRASTIVE GRAPHEMES

A final interesting effect of the significance of emic contrast in the development of the system may be seen in the histories of *'aleph*, *lamed*, and *mem*: since these graphemes were not in minimal contrast with any other, they were free to evolve a large number of very different reflexes.

For example, *'aleph* in its stage 1 form (fig. 10) was so different from all the other square graphemes that it developed forms that eliminated some of the differences, thereby bringing it into greater harmony with the surrounding graphemes. Thus we find the stage 2 form in the Nuremberg Maḥzor (South Germany, 1331), and the variant 2a form, which is extremely difficult to distinguish from the combination of *yod* and *vav*, in the highly artistic contemporary Tripartite Maḥzor (South Germany, c.1320). In both cases, of course, there can be no doubt that the cursive is based on the regular square form of stage 1; and a form similar to the Nuremberg stage 2 is obviously the ancestor of modern Hebrew/Yiddish stage 3.[8]

Because it was the only grapheme rising above the line, *lamed* developed unfettered by problems of minimal contrast. Most of its numerous forms simply take advantage of its obvious distinguishing feature and reduce the rest of the grapheme to a small curve or less (fig. 11). Moreover, there arose quite early the tendency of writing *lamed* as little more than a long straight line, and ultimately this led to possible confusion with the evolving forms of *vav* and word-final *nun* (fig. 7), causing a reinterpretation of the emic contrasts that resulted in the current looped Hebrew/Yiddish form.

Similarly, *mem* had a great deal of freedom in its evolution because of the absence of minimal contrasts. The early medieval square (fig. 12) seems to have been interpreted as two verticals and a (or, ANY) connecting horizontal, and a wide variety of manifestations finally produced the modern cursive.

2. IMPLICATIONS FOR DIACHRONY

2.1. Movement Toward Greater Efficiency

This explanation of the evolution of Hebrew/Yiddish cursive provides evidence for several issues of general interest in diachronic theory. First, it seems fairly clear that all these developments have increased the efficiency--in the sense of Martinet 1955--of the writing system since the contrasts are now easier to both produce and perceive. The evolution of this branch of Hebrew cursive thus illustrates a synthesis of the views of Diringer (1962:16-17) that scripts "progress" toward utility and simplicity and of Martinet (1964:191) that linguistic systems evolve toward "maximal differentiation," because in this case greater speed makes for greater utility, while the reduction of etic features increases simplicity, as does the maximal differentiation that results from the final contrasts.[9]

2.2. A Possible Push Chain

Second, one result of the loss of short high strokes in *vav* and *nun* (fig. 7) was that at some point (fig. 13, stage 4) cursive *vav* and *nun* became easily confused with cursive *lamed*, which therefore developed a new form (stage 5). This would seem to be a classic push chain as formulated by Martinet; yet many scholars have questioned the reality of the push chain reaction, King (1969:194), for example, saying that it can never exist because it is predicated on gradual change, which generative theory rejects. But the data here suggests two things. First, push chains, like other aspects of economy, involve macro- and micro-systemic tension. For, seen from the vantage point of MICROsystemic *lamed* stage 5 is less efficient than stage 4; but seen from the vantage point of the MACROsystem, the feature loss that produced stage 4 *vav* and *nun* introduced greater efficiency into an entire series, thus making it less costly macrosystemically to move *lamed* to stage 5 than for *lamed* to hold the system at stage 3. And second, gradualness is not a necessary condition for push chains: even if stage 4 *vav* and *nun* had arisen spontaneously, they would have presented the same threat to *lamed* that a gradual change presented and would have necessitated the same reaction--whether gradual or spontaneous.

2.3. Gradualness of Change

In this connection, though, it is significant that all the changes discussed in this paper are,

[8] Thus, the suggestion in Chomsky (1957:88) that cursive *'aleph* is an example of how modern Hebrew/Yiddish cursive "possesses traces of the old Hebrew script"--viz., the pre-Aramaic script--is clearly incorrect.

[9] That reduction of etic features increases simplicity is also consistent with Martinet's view (1964:172-178) that too much redundancy is "costly" because it burdens the memory.

as a matter of fact, gradual--which raises a third issue of interest in diachrony. In this particular evolutionary process all the intermediate stages happen to be documented step by step (e.g., Birnbaum 1954, 1971; Roth and Narkiss 1969). There is no evidence of conscious effort, of social conformity, of prestige. The graphemes seem simply to have evolved--as if on their own--toward more efficient shapes. And while it seems obvious that phonological loss or metathesis can hardly be gradual, this does not mean that NO change can be gradual, especially if gradualness is understood not as random drift, but as conscious or semi-conscious choice of a varient after the fact of its unconscious evolution. Now, much evidence has been mustered against the Neogrammarian and Bloomfieldian belief that sound change is at least partially due to unconscious evolution. But even such important alternative theories as variable competence (e.g., Weinreich, Labov, and Herzog 1968) and child grammar simplification (e.g., Halle 1961, Kiparsky 1968) explain only how a change spreads; they do not explain how a change spreads; they do not explain how the variant arises. In graphemics, however, the emergence of variants through evolution--that is, change by gradual evolution--shows signs of being a "natural" process. Moreover, since the reduction of two perpendicular strokes into one diagonal one is a type of assimilation, it seems significant that the two major changes exhibited in the evolution of Hebrew/Yiddish cursive--assimilation and maximal differentiation--parallel two of the three classifications of natural rules posited for phonology in Schane 1972.[10] Admittedly unclear at this point, however, is whether any significance lies in the fact that the assimilation in the development of this particular writing system is limited to etic features, though it does appear that graphemic merger is less tolerable than its phonemic counterpart; this is surprising since it runs contrary to the intuitive feeling of most people--and indeed the implicit assumption of most investigators of writing--that sloppy handwriting is tolerable because it represents a sign of the second order and can be disambiguated by reference to spoken competence. Despite this uncertainty, when gradual evolution is recognized as a series of small but discrete steps rather than as a continuum, and when the other parallels between graphemics and phonology are taken into consideration, perhaps gradual evolution should again be seen as a possibility in such phonetically "natural" cases as, for example, the change of aspirated stops to affricated stops to fricatives.

2.4. Documentation of Sub-emic Change

Finally, the obvious durability of writing makes it of interest to the historical linguist for two reasons. First, because evidence of non-distinctive change is scarce in phonology since written records only rarely reflect sub-phonemic change, but this is not the case in graphemics where the dynamics of non-distinctive change is easily observed (e.g. figs. 5, 7, 13). And second, because the preservation of non-distinctive changes may provide insights into the question of the direction of change, since it allows us to simultaneously observe the change in progress and know its ultimate direction, a situation not normally true in phonology.

3. SUMMARY

At the risk of sometimes belaboring the obvious, this paper has argued that a strict linguistic methodology can provide insights into the history of Hebrew cursive script and that insights from graphemics have implications for diachronic theory generally. It is not suggested that the experience of Hebrew cursive reflects the only or the inevitable development of a linguistic system; needless to say, assimilation and maximal differentiation--the two major processes in this case--very often have opposing results, though here they happen to reinforce each other because assimilation was limited to etic features. More research is required to see what, if any, universal or widely applicable tendencies are at work in this instance, but initial investigations of modern American school-hand indicate the possibility of a similar history.[11] At the very least, however, in the case of Hebrew/Yiddish cursive there is clearly a steady evolution toward greater efficiency.

---

[10] Schane's third category--preferred syllable structure--has no readily apparent analog in graphemics.

[11] This is briefly discussed--but from a pedagogical rather than linguistic viewpoint--in Minkoff (1975).

APPENDIX

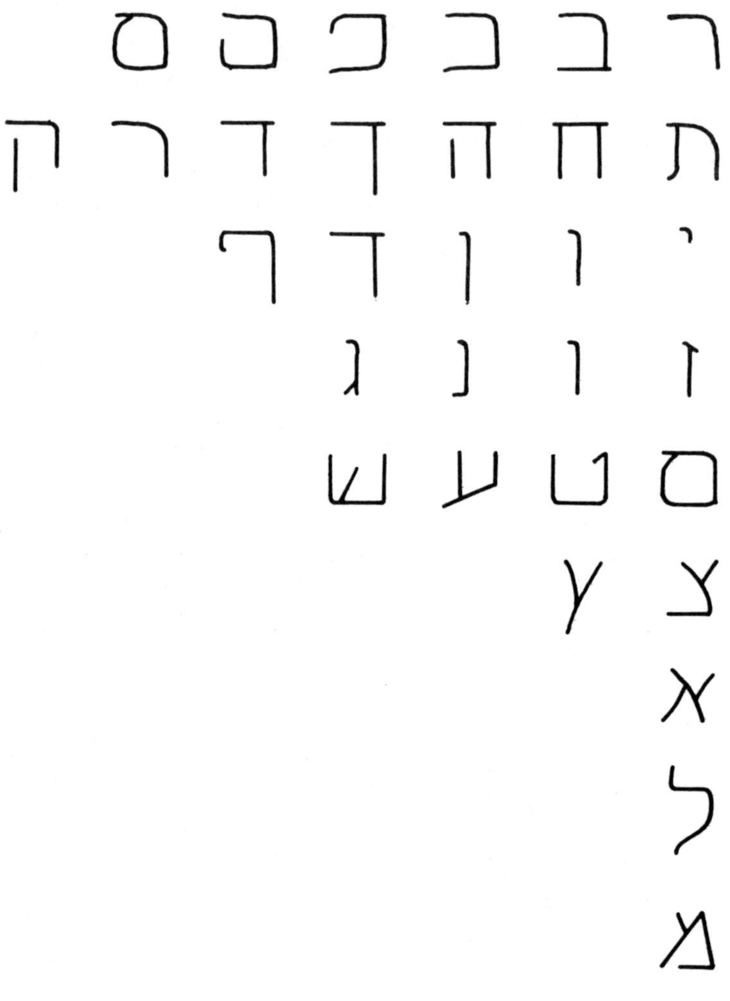

Fig. 1. Modern square graphemes arranged in minimal and nearly minimal pairs. (Some graphemes appear more than once.)

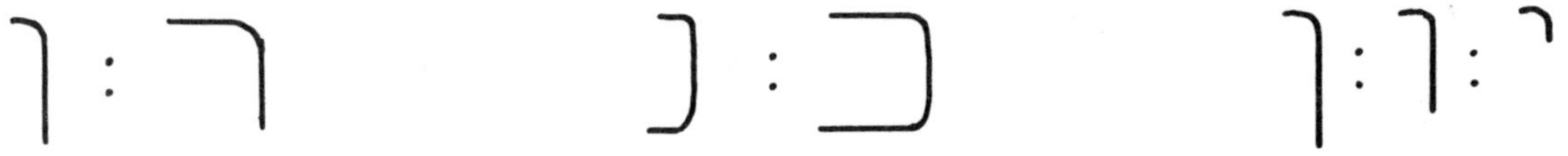

Fig. 2. Minimal pairs based on stroke length.

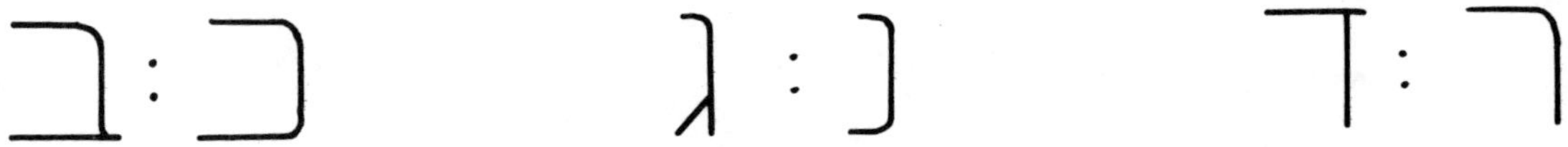

Fig. 3. Minimal pairs based on type of corner.

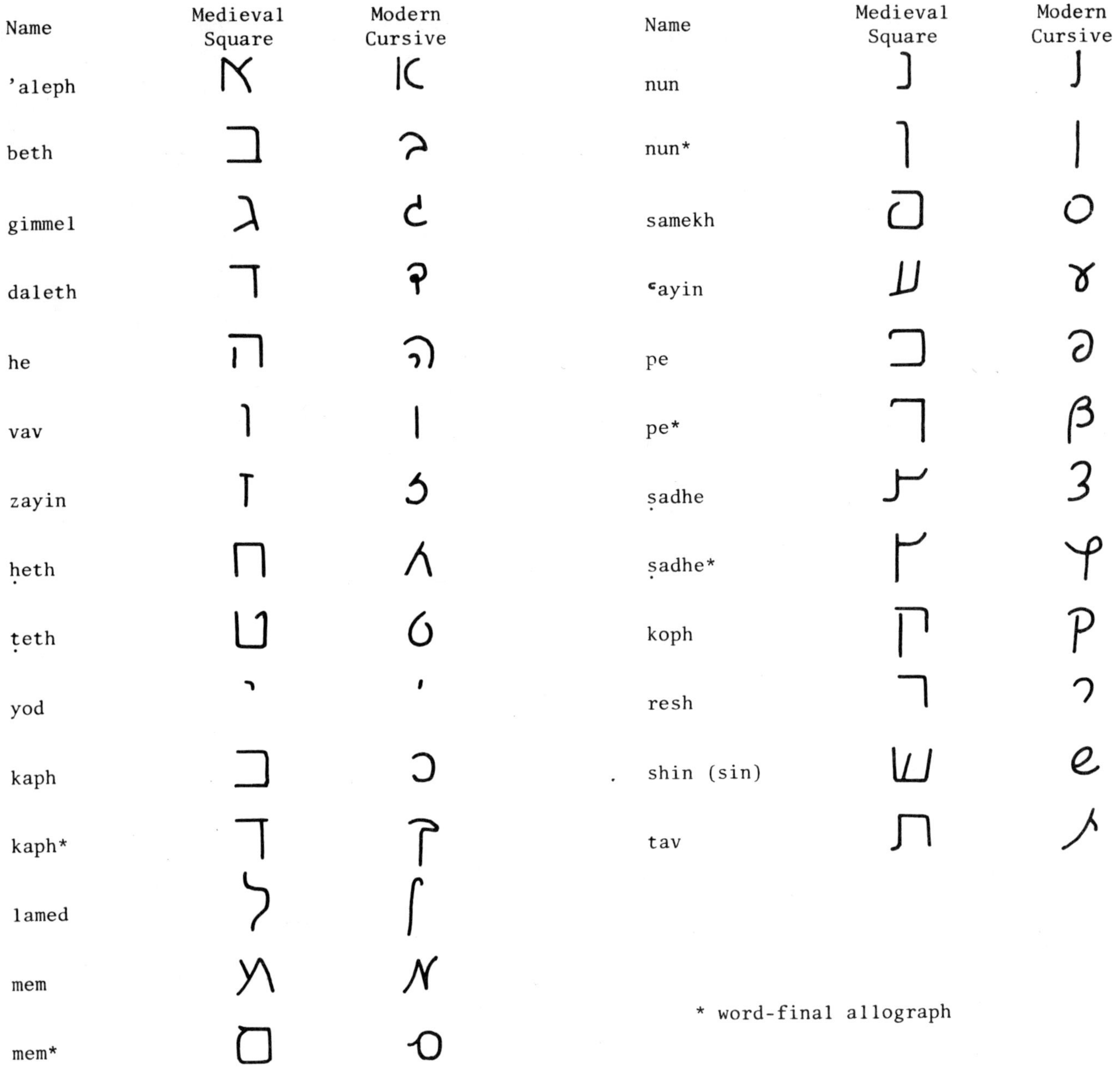

Fig. 4. Medieval square graphemes and their modern cursive reflexes.

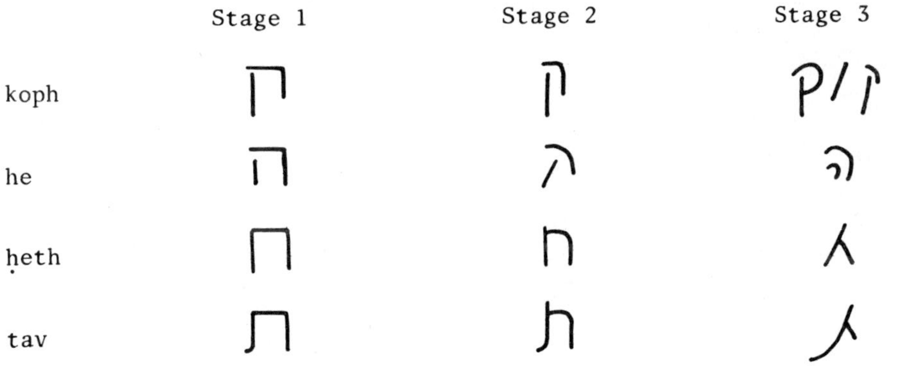

Fig. 5. Evolution of diagonals and curves in *koph, he, ḥeth* and *tav*.

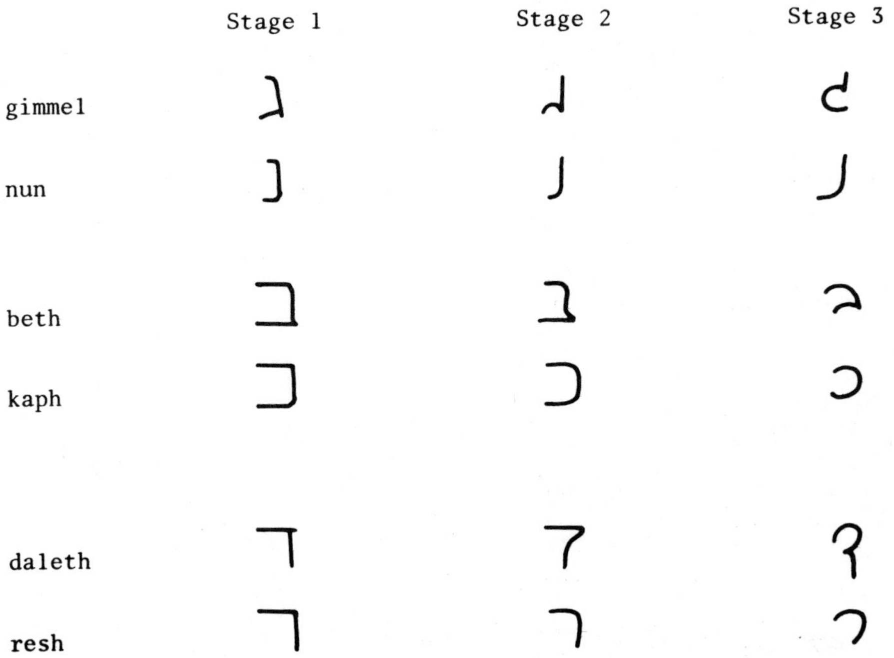

Fig. 6. Distortion of emic contrasts in type of corner.

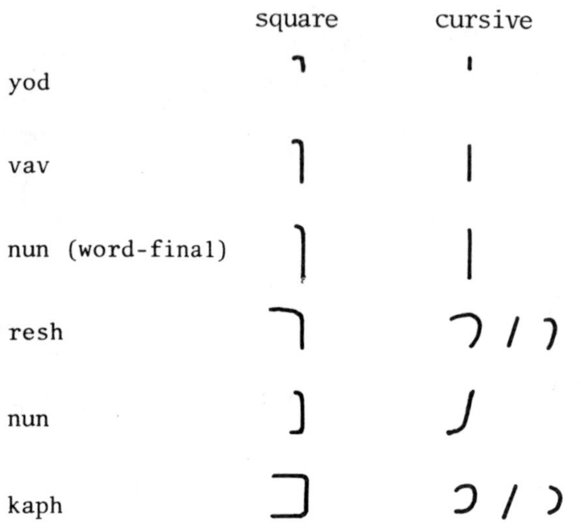

Fig. 7. Systemic loss of short high horizontals; reinterpretation of regular high horizontals.

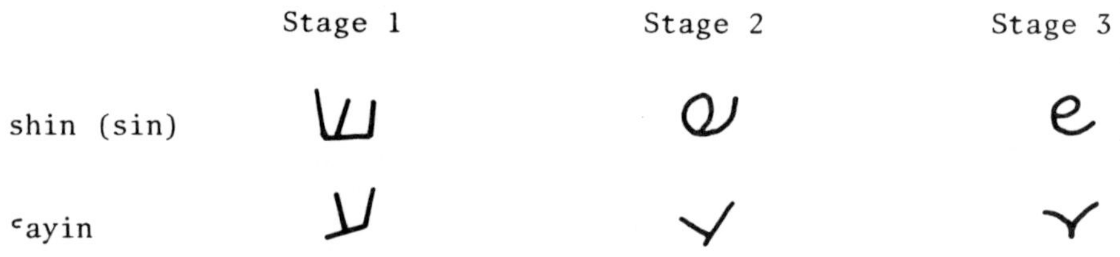

Fig. 8. Evolution of *shin* and ᶜ*ayin*.

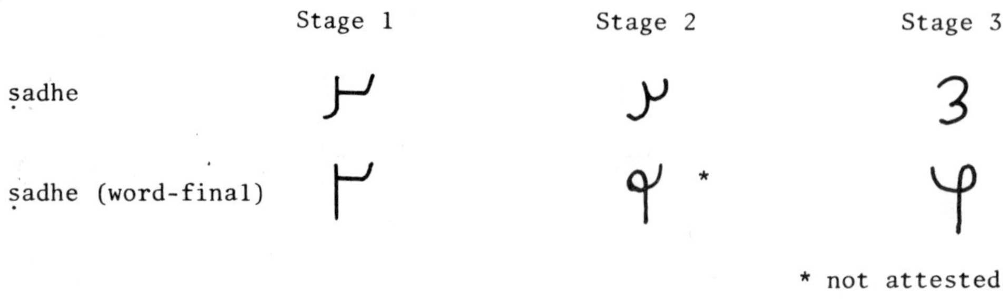

Fig. 9. Evolution of cursive *ṣadhe*.

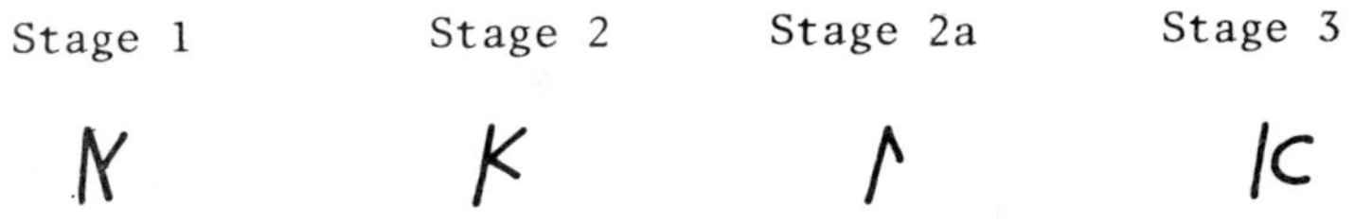

Fig. 10. Evolution of cursive *'aleph*.

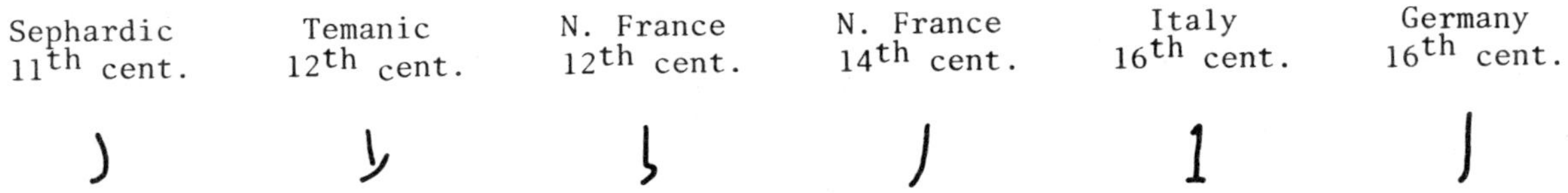

Fig. 11. Forms of *lamed*.

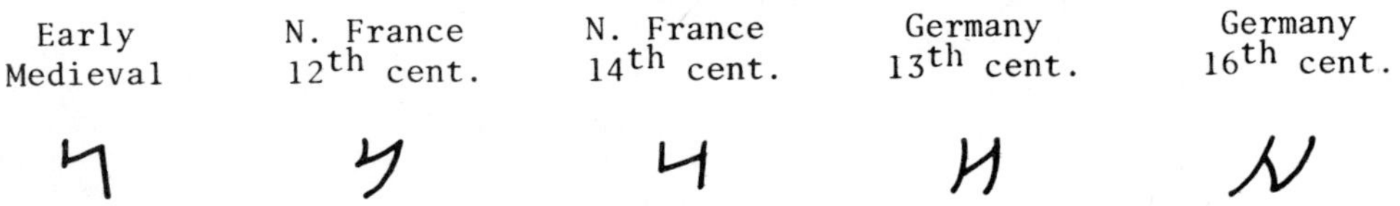

Fig. 12. Forms involved in the evolution of modern cursive *mem*.

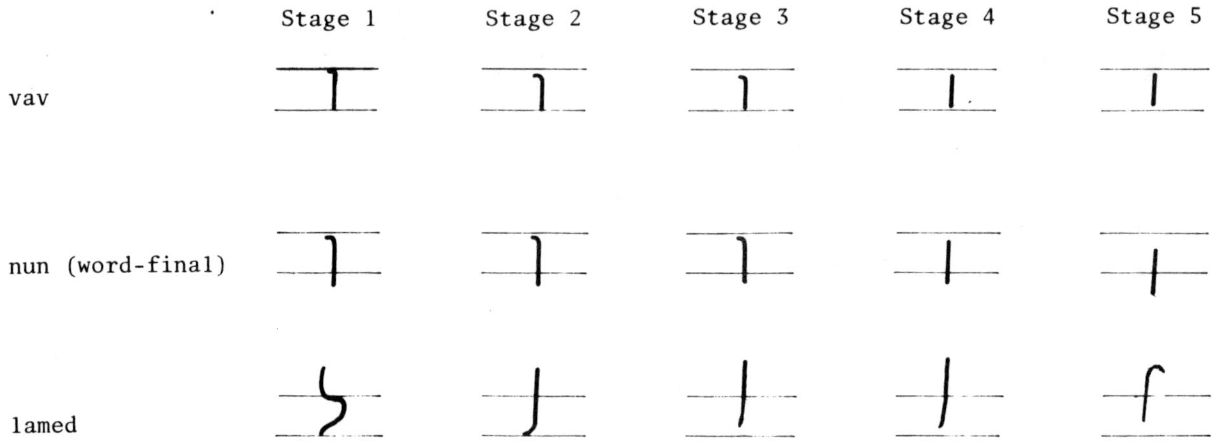

Fig. 13. Push chain effect in the evolution of modern cursive *lamed*.

REFERENCES

Allén, Sture. 1965. *Grafematisk analys som grundval för textedering.* (Nordistica gothoburgensia, Acta Universitatis Gothoburgensia.) Göteborg.

Austin, William, ed. 1967. *Papers in linguistics in honor of Léon Dostert.* (Janua Linguarum, studia memoriae, series maior 25.) The Hague: Mouton.

Bazel, C.E. 1956. "The grapheme," *Litera* 3:43-46. Reprinted in Hamp et al. 1966, 359-361.

Birnbaum, Solomon A. 1954. *The Hebrew scripts.* New York: Humanities Press.

__________. 1971. "Alphabet, Hebrew," *Encyclopaedia Judaica.* 696-743. New York: Macmillan.

Chomsky, William. 1957. *Hebrew: The eternal language.* Philadelphia: Jewish Publication Society.

Diringer, David. 1962. *Writing.* New York: Frederick A. Praeger.

Eden, Murray. 1961. "On the formalization of handwriting," in Jakobson 1961b, 83-88.

Gleason, Henry A. 1961. *Introduction to descriptive linguistics.* Second edition. New York: Holt.

Haas, W., ed. 1969. *Alphabets for English.* Manchester: University Press.

_____. 1970. *Phono-graphic translation.* Manchester: University Press.

Halle, Morris. 1961. "On the role of simplicity in linguistic descriptions," in Jakobson 1961b, 89-94.

Hammarström, Göran. 1964. "Type et typème, graphe et graphème," *Studia neophilologica.* 36:332-340.

__________. 1968. Review of Allén 1965. *Language* 44:907-912.

__________. 1972. "Graphemes and nuncemes of English," *Studia linguistica* 26:14-25.

Hamp, Eric, Fred Householder, Robert Austerlitz, eds. 1966. *Readings in linguistics* II. Chicago: University Press.

Hill, A.A. 1967. "The typology of writing systems," in Austin 1967, 92-99.

Hockett, Charles F. 1958. *A course in modern linguistics.* New York: Macmillan.

Jakobson, Roman. 1961a. "Linguistics and communication theory," in Jakobson 1961b, 245-252.

________, ed. 1961b. *Structure of language and its mathematical aspects.* (Proceedings of Symposia in Applied Mathematics XII.) Providence: American Mathematical Society.

King, Robert. 1969. *Historical linguistics and generative grammar.* Englewood Cliffs, N.J.: Prentice-Hall.

Kiparsky, Paul. 1968. "Linguistic universals and language change," *Universals in linguistic theory,* ed. by Emmon Bach and Robert Harms, 171-202. New York: Holt.

Kyes, Robert. 1970. Review of *Graphematische Untersuchungen zum frühneuhochdeutschen,* by I.T. Piirainen. *Language* 46:193-202.

Martinet, André. 1955. *Économie des changements phonétiques.* Berne: Francke.

________. 1964. *Elements of general linguistics.* London: Faber.

Minkoff, Harvey. 1973a. "A feature analysis of the development of medieval Hebrew scripts," a paper presented at the First North American Conference on Semitic Linguistics.

______________. 1973b. "Some implications of graphemics to diachronic theory." a paper to the Linguistic Society of America.

______________. 1975. "Teaching the transition from print to script analytically," *Elementary English*, 52:203-4.

Pulgram, Ernst. 1951. "Phoneme and grapheme: A parallel," *Word* 7:15-20.

Roth, Cecil and Bezalel Narkiss. 1969. *Hebrew illuminated manuscripts*. New York: Macmillan.

Schane, Sanford A. 1972. "Natural rules in phonology," *Linguistic change and generative theory*, ed. by Robert Stockwell and Ronald Macauley, 199-229. Bloomington: Indiana University Press.

Uldall, H.J. 1944. "Speech and writing," *Acta linguistica* 4:11-16. Reprinted in Hamp et al. 1966, 147-151.

Vachek, Josef. 1945-49. "Some remarks on writing and phonetic transcription," *Acta linguistica* 5:86-93.

____________. 1972. *Written language*. (Janua Linguarum, series critica 14.) The Hague: Mouton.

____________. 1973. Review of Haas 1969, 1970. *Language* 49:190-194.

Venezky, Richard L. 1970. *The structure of English orthography*. (Janua Linguarum, series minor 82.) The Hague: Mouton.

Walsh, John. 1964. "Linguistic factors in the evolution of the alphabet," *Proceedings of the Ninth International Congress of Linguists*, 519-520. The Hague: Mouton.

Weinreich, Uriel, William Labov, Marvin Herzog. 1968. "Empirical foundations for a theory of language change," *Directions for historical linguistics*, ed. by W.P. Lehmann and Yaakov Malkiel, 97-188. Austin: University of Texas Press.

Weir, Ruth H. 1967. "Some thoughts on spelling," in Austin 1967, 169-177.